US Department of
Transportation
Research and
Special Programs
Administration

Morristown NHP
Alternative Transportation System
Planning Study

December 2001

Prepared for
Morristown National Historical Park
Morristown, New Jersey

Prepared by:
John A. Volpe
National Transportation
Systems Center
Kendall Square
Cambridge, MA 02142

REPORT DOCUMENTATION PAGE		Form Approved OMB No. 0704-0188

The public reporting burden for this collection of information is estimated to average 1 hour per response, including the time for reviewing instructions, searching existing data sources, gathering and maintaining the data needed, and completing and reviewing the collection of information. Send comments regarding this burden estimate or any other aspect of this collection of information, including suggestions for reducing the burden, to Department of Defense, Washington Headquarters Services, Directorate for Information Operations and Reports (0704-0188), 1215 Jefferson Davis Highway, Suite 1204, Arlington, VA 22202-4302. Respondents should be aware that notwithstanding any other provision of law, no person shall be subject to any penalty for failing to comply with a collection of information if it does not display a currently valid OMB control number.
PLEASE DO NOT RETURN YOUR FORM TO THE ABOVE ADDRESS.

1. REPORT DATE (DD-MM-YYYY) 12/2001	2. REPORT TYPE Planning Study	3. DATES COVERED (From - To) NA
4. TITLE AND SUBTITLE Morristown National Historical Park Alternative Transportation System Planning Study		5a. CONTRACT NUMBER NA
		5b. GRANT NUMBER NA
		5c. PROGRAM ELEMENT NUMBER NA
6. AUTHOR(S) Jeffrey Bryan, David Spiller, Bill Giezentanner, Cassandra Allwell		5d. PROJECT NUMBER PMIS 89903
		5e. TASK NUMBER NPS TIC No. D-150
		5f. WORK UNIT NUMBER NA
7. PERFORMING ORGANIZATION NAME(S) AND ADDRESS(ES) U.S. Department of Transportation Research and Special Programs Administration John A. Volpe National Transportation Systems Center		8. PERFORMING ORGANIZATION REPORT NUMBER NA
9. SPONSORING/MONITORING AGENCY NAME(S) AND ADDRESS(ES) National Park Service Alternative Transportation Program 1201 Eye St. NW Washington, DC 20005		10. SPONSOR/MONITOR'S ACRONYM(S) WASO/ATP
		11. SPONSOR/MONITOR'S REPORT NUMBER(S) (see 5d. and 5e. above)

12. DISTRIBUTION/AVAILABILITY STATEMENT
Public distribution/availability.

13. SUPPLEMENTARY NOTES
This report addresses alternative transportation decision factors as indicated below (Y/N/NA):
(N) Non-construction options; (Y) park carrying capacity; (Y) life-cycle/ops. & maintenance costs; (Y) cost-effectiveness.

14. ABSTRACT
This alternative transportation plan aims to define a more efficient transit plan for visitors to Morristown. Goals include protecting environmental resources, improving visitor experiences and safety, maximizing use of infrastructure, ensuring compatibility of goals between the park and the surrounding community, and determining cost-effective means to maximize ridership. The report identifies three transportation alternatives for Morristown and analyzes their respective benefits in terms of ridership, safety, visitor enjoyment, and efficiency, as well as costs of each plan.

15. SUBJECT TERMS
Morristown National Historical Park, Alternative Transportation Program, Community Relations, Bus, Visitor Enjoyment, Automobile management

16. SECURITY CLASSIFICATION OF:			17. LIMITATION OF ABSTRACT	18. NUMBER OF PAGES	19a. NAME OF RESPONSIBLE PERSON Gary T. Ritter
a. REPORT	b. ABSTRACT	c. THIS PAGE			
None	None	None	NA	39	19b. TELEPHONE NUMBER (Include area code) 617-494-2716, ritter@volpe.dot.gov

Standard Form 298 (Rev. 8/98)
Prescribed by ANSI Std. Z39.18

Table of Contents

Executive Summary 4

1. Introduction 6

2. Overview of Local Conditions 8
    2.1   Region and Study Area 8
    2.2   Morristown National Historical Park 8
    2.3   Other Cultural Resources 11
    2.4   Transportation Overview 13
    2.5   Morristown NHP Visitation 14
    2.6   Intercept Parking 16

3. Transportation Alternatives 17
    3.1   ATS Route Configuration 17
    3.2   ATS Operating Characteristics 23
    3.3   Comparison of Transportation Alternatives 30
    3.4   Funding Requirements 32
    3.5   Vehicle Options 32

4. System Management 36

5. Next Steps 39

Appendix A - Glossary of Terms 40

Appendix B – Operating Parameters 41

Appendix C – Cycle Time and Minimum Fleet Size Calculations 42

Appendix D – Dwell Time Calculations 43

Volpe National Transportation Systems Center

List of Figures

Figure 1. Average Monthly Visitation 9
Figure 2. Ford Mansion 10
Figure 3. Park Museum 10
Figure 4. Fort Nonsense 10
Figure 5. Wick House 11
Figure 6. Jockey Hollow Visitor Center 11
Figure 7. Jockey Holley Interpretive Loops 19
Figure 8. Town-wide Loop 21
Figure 9. Specialty Vehicles 5000 Series 33
Figure 10. EV22T Manufactured by EVI (E-bus)Electric 33
Figure 11. Chance Coach American Heritage Streetcar, Diesel and CNG options 34
Figure 12. DuponTrolley, Diesel 34
Figure 13. Trolley Enterprises, Electric, Hybrid, and Propane Options 35
Figure 14. Holland Bus Company, Diesel 35

List of Tables

Table 1. New Jersey Transit Ridership 13
Table 2. Annual Visitation 15
Table 3. Adjusted Annual Visitation 15
Table 4. Average Daily Visitation 16
Table 5. ATS passenger flow capacity as percent of Average Day Visitation 28
Table 6. Hourly Percent Occupancy – Parking Facilities 16
Table 7. Operating Parameters - Jockey Hollow Interpretative Loop 24
Table 8. Performance Metrics - Jockey Hollow Interpretative Loop 24
Table 9: Operating Parameters - Park Circuit (Summer Route) 25
Table 10. Performance Metrics - Park Circuit (Summer Route) 26
Table 11. Operating Parameters - Park Circuit (Winter Route) 27
Table 12. Performance Metrics - Park Circuit (Winter Route) 27
Table 13. Operating Parameters - Local Circuit 29
Table 14. Performance Metrics - ATS Local Circuit 29
Table 15. Choose By Advantage 30
Table 16. Vehicle Capital and Operating and Maintenance Costs 32
Table 17. Costs of Management Options 36

Volpe National Transportation Systems Center

EXECUTIVE SUMMARY

On behalf of the Morristown National Historical Park (Park), the Volpe National Transportation Systems Center conducted an Alternative Transportation System (ATS) Planning Study to define and evaluate alternatives for providing public transit for visitors to the Park and other cultural and Historical sites in Morristown, New Jersey.

The 1973 General Management Plan for the Park proposed a shuttle bus system to serve the Jockey Hollow Encampment area, but none was implemented. The need for an alternative means of experiencing the Park that motivated the 1973 proposal is even more pronounced in 2001. Housing and business development in Morristown, and nearby areas, has had a large impact on land use and traffic patterns. An unreported number of vehicles using the Park roads are commuters trying to avoid congestion on local roads, rather than visitors to the Park. The combination of one-way roads, heavy traffic, and complicated intersections spoils visitors' experience and discourages them from exploring the Park and Morristown's many cultural and Historical sites.

The objectives of the proposed ATS alternatives are to:
- Maximize protection of Park and local Historical and environmental resources.
- Improve visitor safety and enhance the visitor's experience through integration of discrete Park units consistent with the interpretative program.
- Maximize use of existing public infrastructure and programs.
- Maximize public-private benefits to facilitate equitable cost sharing.
- Maximize cost-effectiveness (i.e., maximum ridership at minimum life-cycle cost).
- Ensure compatibility of the design with Morristown and Morris County goals of economic development, connecting the community to downtown transit opportunities, and tourism enhancement.
- Create an integrated design, but one that allows maximum autonomy to proceed independently in implementing elements, which service the Park's interests.

This study proposes three alternatives for further consideration: Jockey Hollow Interpretive Loop, Town-wide Loop, and Parking Shuttle Loop. Brief descriptions of the three proposed alternatives are provided below, while more detailed descriptions and maps are provided in the proceeding sections of the study.

- **Jockey Hollow Interpretive Loop** This loop is based on the 1973 General Management Plan for the Park recommendation for a shuttle bus system to serve the Jockey Hollow Encampment area. Two potential routes are discussed, a short and a long route. The main feature of these loops is the ability for the Park to provide interpretation of the Park units. Interpretation could be provided both on the vehicle (by the driver), and at the Park unit. This closed-system would allow for the Park to convey a concise history of the Park units.

- **Town-wide Loop** The town-wide loop includes two separate circuits: a park circuit and a local circuit. The park circuit connects the Park units with other cultural and Historical sites in Morristown, including the Central Business District, hotels, employment centers, and other parks and museums. Integration with the region would attract more ridership, and potentially create partnership opportunities with regional partners for operating the ATS. Interpretation could be provided on the vehicle, but the interpretation would expand to convey the significance of all the units over the years, rather than a concise story. The local circuit services sites in Morristown, but does not include any park units.

- **Parking Shuttle Loop**   The parking shuttle loop connects various parking facilities within the center of Morristown that are recommended to be designated as 'intercept' parking facilities. The Parking Shuttle Loop would collect and distribute residents and visitors to and from these facilities and bring them to the main 'transportation hub' for access to the ATS.

The Park needs to decide whether they want to assume the operations and maintenance of a transit system, contract for the ATS, or partner with a local government agency or public/private entity. This study presents four management options:

- **Morristown NHP purchases the vehicles and hires permanent or term employees as drivers** This option is similar to the successful Lowell NHP program and offers interpretative advantages.

- **Contracting to a third party to provide vehicles, drivers, and maintenance**   This option is not seen to be viable due to funding limits.

- **NPS buys the equipment, then obtains drivers and maintenance through a service contract(s)**   This option is not seen to be viable given the potential lack of savings with large operators and uncertainty about the costs and reliability of a smaller or new operation.

- **Partnering with a local government agency or a public-private organization**   This option has many advantages, but potential funding sources need to be further researched.

The Park and local stakeholders are interested in planning and conducting a pilot program to test the feasibility of an ATS for Morristown. Results from the pilot program will provide guidance to the Park and local stakeholders regarding which route alternatives and management options are financially feasible and will achieve the desired outcomes.

1. INTRODUCTION

The nation's first National Historical Park is located in and around Morristown, New Jersey. Morristown is located in north-central New Jersey, thirty miles from New York City. The Morristown National Historical Park (Park) consists of four units that played important roles during the Revolutionary War—Washington Headquarters, Fort Nonsense, Jockey Hollow Encampment Area, and New Jersey Brigade Encampment. These units provide a unique opportunity for visitors to enter into the lives of Revolutionary War soldiers and local villagers as they survived two grim winter encampments and prepared to meet the British army.

The Park attracts approximately 536,000 visitors annually[1]. The Park depends heavily on access by private vehicles. The current reliance on private automobiles for unit access adds approximately 174,000 vehicles per year to local traffic, contributes to noise and air pollution, and increases the risk of accidents. On an average weekend day during peak visitation months, Park visitors may account for more than 1,350 vehicles.[2] Morristown and Morris County are struggling to cope with increasing traffic. Several efforts are underway to explore regional transit services and re-routing of traffic through Morristown's Central Business District (CBD).

The combination of one-way roads, heavy traffic, and complicated intersections makes arrival at the Washington Headquarters unit very difficult, confusing, and even dangerous for out-of-town visitors. Frustration with traffic congestion and difficulty navigating between the units, results in many visitors cutting short their visits before they have seen all of the units. A sustainable Alternative Transportation System (ATS) would make a visit to these units more enjoyable and facilitate the Park's efforts to provide quality interpretation of their Historical significance.

An ATS for the Park that is integrated with transit services serving other community needs could contribute to the sustainability of Park operations, help protect Park resources, and contribute to the efforts of local government to meet the needs of its residents, employees, and visitors. Providing a convenient means of traveling among the units would provide visitors with an expanded opportunity to understand the importance of the units. In addition to facilitating movement between the units, an ATS can deliver interpretive narration or other informational media presentations that explain the units and their relationships with each other and to the community.

The Volpe National Transportation Systems Center has prepared this study for the National Park Service (NPS) to address the following objectives:

- Maximize protection of Park and local Historical and environmental resources.
- Improve visitor safety and enhance the visitor's experience through integration of discrete Park units consistent with the interpretative program.
- Maximize use of existing public infrastructure and programs.
- Maximize public-private benefits to facilitate equitable cost sharing.
- Maximize cost-effectiveness (i.e., maximum ridership at minimum life-cycle cost).

---

[1] Average visitation for 1997, 1998, 1999, and 2000. Source National Park Service, Public Use Statistics Office.
[2] Computed by dividing peak month visitation in half to obtain weekend visitation and dividing weekend visitation by eight to obtain average weekend day visitation then dividing by 2.6 passengers per vehicle to obtain the number of vehicles. The passengers per vehicle (2.6) is an assumption made by NPS.

Volpe National Transportation Systems Center

- Ensure compatibility of the design with Morristown and Morris County goals of economic development, connecting the community to downtown transit opportunities, and tourism enhancement.
- Create an integrated design, but one that allows maximum autonomy to proceed independently in implementing elements, which service the Park's interests.

The focus of the this study is on transportation needs specific to the Park, however, the potential for integration within a broader network of local and regional public transportation services is considered appropriate to the early phase of ATS planning. The relationship of an ATS to the area's larger transportation needs could be addressed in more detail as part of a subsequent NPS study or regional planning effort.

Subsequent sections of this study present the study findings. Chapter 2 provides an overview of local conditions, including land use, the Park, and other cultural and Historical sites. Chapter 3 identifies potential ATS alternatives, in terms of the configuration of potential routes and service operating characteristics, such as headways and vehicle fleet size. Chapter 4 discusses options for managing the ATS. In conclusion, Chapter 5 outlines next steps of ATS planning for the Park and local stakeholders.

2. OVERVIEW OF LOCAL CONDITIONS

2.1 Region and Study Area

The Park is located in Morristown, Morris Township, and Harding Township, New Jersey. It is less than 30 miles west of New York City in Morris County on Interstate Route 287. It is located in the center of the northern portion of the Interstate 95 corridor, running from Washington, DC to Boston – 220 miles from Washington DC, 82 miles from Philadelphia, 142 miles from Hartford, and 250 miles from Boston.

The region has experienced tremendous socioeconomic change during the last thirty years. Until the post WWII era, it was an area of large estates and horse farms. In 1970, almost eight percent of the county was farmland, compared to two percent of the county in 1995. Despite significant development, more than half of Morris County remains forest or wetlands. Morris County has rolling hills, stream valleys, swamps, small mountains, and a wealth of Historical and cultural attractions.

Morristown has a fulltime population of approximately 17,000 people, and a daytime population of nearly 75,000 people. Although designated as a Regional Center by the 2000 New Jersey State Development and Redevelopment Plan, Morristown is also a tree-lined bedroom suburb of New York City, and a growing employment center. Some of the area's largest employers include Lucent Technologies (5,094 employees), Morristown Memorial Hospital (4,200 employees), AT&T (4,200 employees) and the County of Morris (2,800 employees). Congested arterial routes and a CBD are a result of the high volume of activity. The CBD attracts considerable traffic throughout the day with people commuting to work, frequenting hundreds of businesses, and dining in the numerous restaurants.

The region has considerable potential as a tourist destination due to its rich diversity of cultural and recreational attractions. Currently there are three hotels in Morristown (Best Western Hotel, Headquarters Plaza Hotel, and the Westin Hotel), which have a total of 515 rooms; a fourth hotel (The Inn at Vail Mansion) is scheduled to open by 2003 with 101 rooms. The hotels report that they operate, on average, at approximately 75 percent capacity. Corporate travelers are the primary customers. Special events, such as weddings, are the mainstay of the hotels' weekend business. An easy to use, convenient ATS that provides access to the area's attractions from the Morristown Green and the hotels would encourage hotel guests to explore Morristown and the Park units.

2.2 Morristown National Historical Park

Morristown served as winter encampments for General George Washington and the Continental Army in 1777 and 1779. During the Revolutionary War, General Washington chose Morristown for his winter encampment because it was close enough to keep watch on William Howe's Redcoats in New York City, but protected enough by the Watchung Mountains to the east as to be defensible. In January of 1777, the Continental Army - numbering about 1900 - trudged into town fresh from victories over the British at Trenton and Princeton to rest and refill its depleted ranks. The surrounding countryside offered provisions from nearby farms and critical supplies of iron and gunpowder. The surrounding forests offered building materials, wild game, and firewood. General Washington stayed at the Arnold Tavern on the Morristown Green while his troops camped nearby, and lodged in local homes.

Volpe National Transportation Systems Center

Washington chose Morristown again for the winter of 1778-1779. It turned out to be the hardest winter of the century. The army of 10,000 troop and 2,000 women and children camp followers, had grown too large to be accommodated in and around the town and a site about three miles southwest of the Morristown Green called Jockey Hollow was used for the encampment. Mrs. Jacob Ford, Jr. offered Washington, his wife and several officers' quarters in Morristown's finest house, the Ford Mansion.

In 1933, Congress designated lands and properties in the Morristown area as the first National Historical Park in the NPS. Its purpose is to preserve the lands and cultural features associated with the grim winter encampments that tested the leadership of General Washington and the resolve of the troops. The three original units of the Park are Washington's Headquarters, Fort Nonsense, and Jockey Hollow Encampment Area. In 1974, the New Jersey Brigade Encampment Area was added to the Park. Today, the four units of the Park collectively attract approximately 536,000 visitors per year. As shown on the figure below, visitation peaks between May and October with between 50,000 and 60,000 visitors. Only January and December drop below 30,000 visitors. Relative to many other parks, this is a fairly stable visitation. Figure 1[3] presents the average monthly visitation for the Years 1997, 1998, 1999, and 2000.

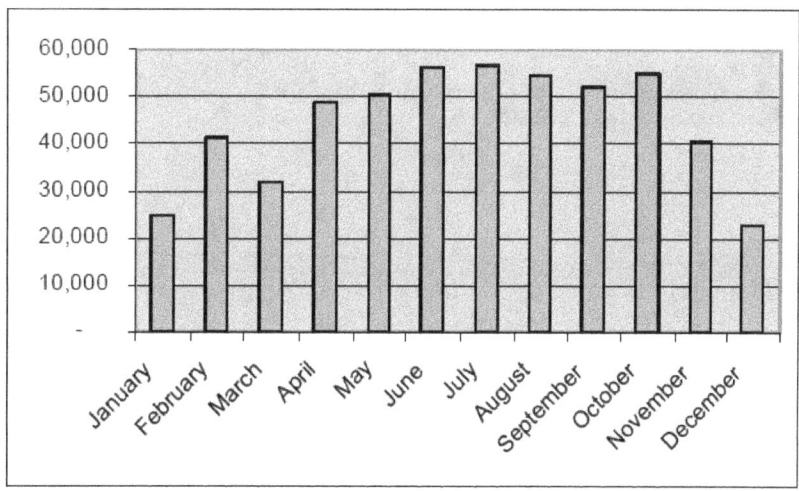

Figure 1. Average Monthly Visitation

---

[3] Source National Park Service, Public Use Statistics Office.

Volpe National Transportation Systems Center

The **Washington Headquarters** unit (12 acres) consists of the Ford Mansion (1772) and the Park museum. The Ford Mansion served as the army's headquarters during the winter of 1778-1779. In addition to General and Mrs. Washington, it was also the residence of eighteen of the General's staff and Mrs. Ford and her four daughters. Tours of the house are offered 362 days of the year.

Figure 2. Ford Mansion

Figure 3. Park Museum

The Park museum, designed by John Russell Pope, houses exhibits of military and other artifacts that provide glimpses into the lives of the Continental Army in its winter quarters. The museum is an important orientation point for the events that occurred in Morristown during the Revolutionary War and the lives of local residents. A 9,00 square feet expansion of the museum is scheduled to be complete by 2005.

Fort Nonsense (35 acres) is located approximately one mile west of Washington's Headquarters on a steep hill overlooking the town. In May of 1777, General Washington ordered his troops to dig trenches and raise embankments on the crest of the hill to provide a strategic location to protect the town and provide distant views to the east. The earthworks, or redoubt as Washington called it, became know as "Fort Nonsense" by 1790 because of a legend that the fortifications had been ordered only to keep the troops busy.

Figure 4. Fort Nonsense

Volpe National Transportation Systems Center

The **Jockey Hollow Encampment Area** (1,320 acres) lies approximately 3 miles southwest of Fort Nonsense. It includes the location of the "log house city" constructed by the approximately 10,000 troops from Massachusetts, Rhode Island, Connecticut, New York, Maryland, Pennsylvania, and Canada. It also is the site of the Jockey Hollow Visitor Center and the Wick House, which served as General Arthur St. Clair's residence and headquarters.

Figure 5. Wick House

The **New Jersey Brigade Encampment Area** (321 acres), one mile southwest of Jockey Hollow, was the winter home to the approximately 900 troops from New Jersey. It also includes several 20th century buildings used for various park functions and the Cross Estate Gardens, which are open to the public.

Figure 6. Jockey Hollow Visitor Center

2.3 Other Cultural Resources

Morristown and Morris County are rich in other cultural and recreational resources that could enhance the desirability of the region as a tourism destination. In addition to the Park, there are numerous museums, cultural facilities, recreational areas, and Historical sites. The area is also aggressively developing a network of walking and biking trails. The following is a list and short description of some of the sites that could be included in a visit to Morristown and potentially could be linked by an ATS. Visitation data[4] are also provided for some of the sites.

Morristown and Morris Township

Acorn Hall This 1853 residence, with its Victorian gardens and gift shop, is the headquarters of the Morris County Historical Society. It is furnished with original examples of Victoriana. Location: 68 Morris Avenue in Morristown (less than a quarter of a mile from Washington's Headquarters). Annual visitation is 1,538.

Fosterfields Living Historical Farm This working farm and Historical house represent farming and estate living in the 1880 to 1927 time period. Visitors experience life in this era through demonstrations by interpreters in Historical dress. Location: 73 Kahdena Road in Morristown. Annual visitation is 20, 925.

---

[4] Visitation data provided by the Historical Morris Visitors Center. Numbers reflect the average annual visitation from 1998 – 2000.

Volpe National Transportation Systems Center

Historical Speedwell This National Historical Landmark was the home of Stephen Vail, owner of the Speedwell Iron Works. It was also where Alfred Vail and Samuel Morse developed the telegraph. Location: 333 Speedwell Avenue in Morristown. Annual visitation is 1,445.

Macculloch Hall Historical Museum and Gardens This 20-room Federal-style mansion was built in 1810 by George Macculloch, the father of the 1831 Morris Canal. Rooms display 18th and 19th century furnishings and changing exhibits. Location: 45 Macculloch Avenue in Morristown. Annual visitation is 4,268.

The Morris Museum This art museum features permanent and changing exhibitions. Location: 6 Normandy Heights Road in Morristown. Annual visitation is 198,067.

Schuyler Hamilton House Museum The colonial home of Dr. Jabez Campfield was used by General Washington's personal physician, Dr. John Cochrane. Washington's aid, General Alexander Hamilton, courted houseguest, Betsy Schuyler here. Location: 5 Olyphant Place in Morristown.

Historical Morristown Walking Tour This walking tour connects twenty-four of downtown Morristown's most impressive Historical buildings. It includes Macculloch Hall, the sites of Arnolds Tavern and The Continental Storehouse, and the Morristown Green as well as a number of residences, churches, and public buildings.

Frelinguysen Arboretum The 127-acre site includes a variety of theme gardens – shade, cottage, perennial, rock, and vegetable – as well as specialized collections of shrubs and trees. Visitors can also stop for regularly scheduled shows or events at the Haggerty Education Center. Location: 53 E. Hanover Drive in Morris Township.

Other Nearby Sites

Craftsman Farms The former home of Gustav Stickley, the foremost spokesman for the American Arts and Crafts Movement. The National Historical Register house and its 31-acre site embody the movement's "Design with Nature" philosophy. Location: off Route 10 on Manor Lane in Parsippany, about three miles from the Morristown Green.

Museum of Early Trades and Crafts This museum, housed in a National Register of Historical Places, Romanesque Revival library built in 1899, features a collection of 18th and 19th century tools and craft objects. Active craft projects and demonstrations are also regularly scheduled. Location: on Main Street at Green Village Road in Madison, about three miles from the Morristown Green. Annual visitation is 13,667.

Loantaka Brook Reservation This linear park encompasses more than 570 acres along Loantaka Brook and is adjacent to one of the more populated urbanized areas of the county. There are nearly five miles of trails in the park that provide biking, jogging, hiking, horseback riding and cross-country skiing opportunities. There are also three ball fields. Location: Kitchell Road and South Street in the Townships of Morris, Harding, and Chatham about 2 miles from the Morristown Green. The Loantaka Brook area reputedly served as an encampment site during 1777 for Washington's Continentals.

Volpe National Transportation Systems Center

Patriots Path This more than 20-mile network of bicycling, hiking, and equestrian paths and trails links numerous parks, conservation areas, and Historical sites across Morris County including Frelinghuysen Arboretum, Washington's Headquarters, Fosterfields Living Historical Farm, Jockey Hollow, and Historical Speedwell. Several other nearby paths have been developed and many more pedestrian and bike routes are proposed.

Great Swamp National Wildlife Refuge This area of more than 7,500 acres includes the first designated Wilderness in the United States. There are more than eight miles of trails and three visitor/education centers. The Fish and Wildlife Service, a sister DOI agency, operates the site. Refuge Headquarters is on Pleasant Plains Road in Basking Ridge. Annual visitation is 25,565.

2.4 Transportation Overview

Morristown is struggling with traffic congestion. It is a desirable place to live and work. Large estates have been converted to residential subdivisions and former horse farms have been developed as corporate headquarters. The area has become an employment center as well as a bedroom suburb of New York City. The Morristown Train Station is a major transportation node with parking for commuters. A transit-oriented zoning district has been adopted for an area around the station and a major mixed-use development has been approved. New Jersey Transit Authority (NJT) recently began an electric car-leasing program. Under this program, NJT provides 10 electric vehicle charging "stations" at Morristown Train Station. Individuals and employers lease the electric cars from NJT and park the cars at the Morristown Train Station every night. Commuters into New York City converge on Morristown Train Station and a growing number of reverse commuters arrive at the station and board shuttles provided by local employers or walk to nearby destinations. Many employees of local businesses drive to and from work. Staff and patients of the Morristown Hospital travel to and from the hospital and its affiliated Rehabilitation Center. Out-of-town students attend private schools in Morristown. Shoppers and restaurant-goers come to the many shops and cafes located near the Morristown Green or along South Street. Local residents travel to many of the attractions listed above, to hike, bike, and visit the area's many cultural and Historical sites.

Transit. NJT operates a direct commuter rail route to New York City. The most recent statistics for ridership are provided in Table 1. Eastbound refers to riders who board in Morristown and travel east, towards New York City. Westbound refers to riders who travel west, away from New York City, and alight at the Morristown Train Station. The number of passengers reflects an average daily estimate.

Table 1. New Jersey Transit Ridership

	Eastbound	**Westbound**
Weekday Peak[5]	532 passengers	360 passengers
Weekday Off-Peak[6]	390 passengers	384 passengers
Weekend[7]	731 passengers	485 passengers

---

[5] Average daily estimate fiscal year 2000. AM peak eastbound is 6:30 AM – 9:30 AM. PM peak westbound is 4:15 PM – 7:30 PM. Source NJT Rail Service Planning, Operations Analysis Unit.
[6] Average daily estimate fiscal year 2000. Off-peak eastbound and westbound is 9:31 AM – 4:14 PM. Source NJT Rail Service Planning, Operations Analysis Unit.
[7] Average daily estimate fiscal year 1992. Source NJT Rail Service Planning, Operations Analysis Unit.

NJT estimates that weekday peak ridership consists of commuters (approximately 90 percent) and students (approximately 10 percent). Morristown is also served by bus service provided by Morris County (Metro funded by NJT and others). The only Morristown public transit is a small bus that operates three days per week.

Regional Highways. Interstate Route 287 is the major highway running through Morristown. Its alignment is northeast to southwest, linking Interstate Route 80 in the north to Interstate Route 78 in the south. The Washington Headquarters unit is adjacent to Interstate Route 287 at exit 36, while the Jockey Hollow is more than two miles north of exit 30B.

Major Arterials. Several major arterial routes converge in Morristown. Several of these routes and more local roads provide access to the National Park units.

- New Jersey Route 510, Columbia Road, enters Morristown from the east. Traffic from downtown Morristown heading east moves along Morris Street and passes the Washington Headquarters unit on its way to Columbia Road. Morris Street becomes one-way, east, before it passes the Park unit, while westbound traffic from Columbia Road is diverted onto Lafayette Avenue, one-way, behind the Washington Headquarters unit.
- US Route 202, Speedwell Avenue, comes in to Morristown from the north and continues south as Mount Kemble Avenue. Mount Kemble Avenue is the most direct route between Morristown Green and Jockey Hollow. During rush hours it can be very congested and slow because of commuting traffic to a number of corporate headquarters and to the Morristown Train Station.
- A predominately residential local street, Western Avenue, provides an alternative route from the Morristown Green to Jockey Hollow. Because of traffic on Mount Kemble Avenue, this street is often used as the main route to Jockey Hollow.
- New Jersey Route 24 intersects Interstate Route 287 just north of Morristown. At Morristown Green it becomes Washington Street and then Mendham Road as it heads west to Mendham Township. This route is also slow and congested during rush hours.
- New Jersey Route 124 enters Morristown from the east on Madison Avenue. The Morristown Memorial Hospital, a major traffic generator with needs for employee and patient transportation, is located on Madison Avenue just before it reaches I-287. Just after crossing Interstate Route 287, New Jersey Route 124 becomes South Street, Morristown's major shopping street and ends at Morristown Green where it joins New Jersey Route 24.

2.5 Morristown NHP Visitation

Assessment of the market demand and feasibility of an ATS for Morristown NHP and its gateway community depends critically on current and projected growth in visitation at the Park. It also depends as well on the likelihood that substantial numbers of visitors can be induced to combine visitation of more than one Park unit, now made possible by providing good access and linkage between the Park units.

Annual visitation ("Recreation Visits") for the last three years, as well as the three-year average, is shown in Table 2. It is important to note, however, that the estimate of "Recreation Visits" is a computed value. It is based on measuring vehicles, at the in-bound entrance lane, at the Tempe

Wick and Western Avenue gates, and at the exit lanes at the Fort Nonsense and Cross-Estate gate[8]. A seasonally related passenger occupancy factor is then applied, after adjusting for the expected flow of Park-related vehicles and through-commuters. These counts therefore, do not reflect precise visitation to the Park Unit. This is not the case for Fort Nonsense and at Washington Headquarters. At Fort Nonsense, the access road dead-ends there and the counts are taken at the outbound exit lane. Similarly, at Washington Headquarters the visitation data reflect actual head counts of visits to the Museum on the grounds of the Park Unit.

Table 2. Annual Visitation

Year	Tempe Wick Gate Visitors	Western Ave Gate Visitors	Fort Nonsense Visitors	Cross Estate Gate Visitors	Washington Headquarter Museum Visitors	Total Number of Visitors
1998	224,018	217,234	43,769	20,884	37,372	543,277
1999	212,446	245,461	45,933	33,795	31,012	568,647
2000	226,179	154,181	46,753	29,082	27,653	483,848
3-year Average	220,881	205,625	45,485	27,920	32,012	531,924

Adjusted annual visitation for the three-year average is shown in Table 3. The adjustments are made based on a conservative assumption that 80 percent of the vehicle counts during the month of January represent an underlying commuter flow via the Tempe Wick, Western Avenue and Cross Estate gates. Therefore, only the incremental monthly count of vehicles above this underlying flow level represents actual visitation to the Park.

Table 3. Adjusted Annual Visitation

Year	Tempe Wick Gate Visitors	Western Ave Gate Visitors	Fort Nonsense Visitors	Cross Estate Gate Visitors	Washington Headquarter Museum Visitors	Total Number of Visitors
3-year Average	191,986	178,074	45,485	1,520	32,012	449,077

Estimates of the average daily visitation for the May through October, and November through April operating seasons are provided in Table 4.

---

[8] Discussion with T. Wade, NPS/ WASO-TNT.

Volpe National Transportation Systems Center

Table 4. Average Daily Visitation

Year	Tempe Wick Gate	Western Ave Gate	Fort Nonsense	Cross Estate	Washington Headquarters[9]
May-Oct, 1998	783	730	149	39	92
Nov-April, 1998	462	477	94	77	72
May-Oct, 1999	739	817	163	132	79
Nov-April, 1999	441	547	92	56	64
May-Oct, 2000	793	497	146	88	75
Nov-April, 2000	463	360	114	74	52
3-year average, May-Oct	772	681	153	86	82
3-year average, Nov-April	455	461	100	69	63

2.6 Intercept Parking

The Morristown Parking Authority manages a total of 3,294 parking spaces. Of these spaces, 689 are on-street meters. The remaining 2,605 spaces are in surface lots or parking garages. Three major parking structures, Maple Avenue Deck (204 spaces), the Ann-Bank Garage (495 spaces), and the John L. Dalton Garage (699 spaces) account for 1,398 spaces. Table 5 shows hourly percent occupancy for each of these facilities and for the other parking structures and lots.

Table 5. Hourly Percent Occupancy – Parking Facilities

Parking Structure or Lot	Capacity	8:00 AM	10:00 AM	12:00 N	2:00 PM	4:00 PM	6:00 PM	8:00 PM	9:00 PM
Maple Avenue Deck	204	0%	86%	98%	99%	92%	75%	64%	64%
Dalton Garage	699	4%	25%	18%	16%	11%	5%	9%	7%
Ann-Bank Garage	495	19%	70%	69%	61%	55%	17%	19%	16%
Other	1,207	58%	73%	77%	76%	74%	60%	53%	49%
Total	2,605	32%	61%	62%	59%	55%	39%	36%	33%

Source: Morristown Parking Authority Annual Report – August 2000

These figures indicate that there is considerable excess parking capacity. Plans to add another deck to the Maple Avenue lot will nearly double capacity for that heavily used facility. An ATS could use some or all of the existing public parking facilities (and planned enhancements) as 'intercept' parking facilities. By distributing the 'intercept' parking function to these existing facilities, there is less likelihood of creating a single bottleneck or point of congestion on the local streets. Multiple arterial access routes into Morristown also necessitate a distributed and decentralized design for the 'intercept' parking function. The proposed signage system will aid in identifying and finding these parking facilities

Volpe National Transportation Systems Center

3. TRANSPORTATION ALTERNATIVES

Many National Parks have begun introducing ATS – most notably Zion, Acadia, Cape Cod, and Yosemite have functioning systems, while other parks and cultural sites are planning to implement or expand public transportation systems. In some cases park visitors, driving their individual vehicles, have had adverse impacts on the park or surrounding region's natural or cultural resources. The ATS reduces these impacts and provides a more enjoyable alternative for experiencing the park and receiving interpretive information. In several of these examples use by park visitors has far exceeded planners' estimates.

The 1976 General Management Plan for the Morristown National Historical Park proposed a shuttle bus system to serve the Jockey Hollow Encampment area. Bus pullouts and stops were built but the system was never implemented. The need for an alternative means of experiencing the Park that motivated the 1976 proposal is even more pronounced in 2001. Commuters trying to avoid congestion on local roads are increasingly using the Park roads as a way of traveling to and from work. At the same time, conditions in the community, especially increased traffic congestion, further justify an ATS and provide a rationale for an integrated system that not only addresses the transportation problems of the Park, but helps the community reduce reliance on private vehicles and the overcrowding of local streets they generate. Local community approval and support have been mentioned as major benefits where transit systems have been implemented in other parks.

The Park units depend heavily on access by private vehicles. In recent years about 98 percent of the visits to Jockey Hollow (Tempe Wick Gate) have been visitors arriving by private vehicles. These vehicles carry an average of 2.6^{10} occupants. Visitors to the Park arrive with a desire to explore the Park's Historical features and trails. All too often they are thwarted in their efforts to understand the significance of the scattered Park units. The visitor's experience is interrupted with finding the next unit on unfamiliar roads. This report suggests potential ATS alternatives that have been designed to reduce this overwhelming reliance on the use of private vehicles. An ATS would facilitate more frequent visitation to multiple units within the Park and help provide the visitor with a fuller understanding of the Historical events that occurred in and around Morristown. In addition, an increase in the use of higher occupancy vehicles would decrease the adverse environmental impacts of private vehicles on the Park's resources and throughout the Morristown area. The implementation of a new transportation option would assist in the protection of the Park's natural and cultural resources, improve visitor safety, and enhance the experience of visiting the units. In addition, the implementation of an integrated system in cooperation with local government agencies, would offer Park visitors and local residents increased opportunities to visit other attractions and aid in reducing overall traffic congestion.

3.1 ATS Route Configuration

The study team considered a number of factors to identify alternative route configurations for further analysis. These factors include:
- Connectivity between main activity centers
- Modal and inter-modal transfer opportunities
- Ridership attraction

---

[9] Excludes bus and group visitor counts
[10] Assumption made by National Park Service Public Use Statistics Office.

Volpe National Transportation Systems Center

- Operational considerations (e.g., road and vehicle compatibility, cycle times, provisions for layover, controllability of the route operation)

Attracting riders is key to the success of any ATS. To be attractive to riders the transportation system has to include the desired destinations, be convenient, and be frequent enough that riders do not feel stranded (i.e. headway, or time interval between successive arrivals of transit vehicles at an individual stop, would be approximately 30 minutes). This study does not include ridership demand analyses for an ATS (see Section 2.5 for Morristown NHP visitation and passenger flow capacities at the Park units).

This study proposes three types of loops, which incorporate the design and operational factors listed above in order to attract a 'critical mass' of riders. The loops include the **Jockey Hollow Interpretive Loop**, the **Town-wide Loop**, and a **Parking Shuttle Loop**. The Jockey Hollow interpretive loop is based on the proposal in the 1973 General Management Plan. The town-wide loop is designed to connect important sites in Morristown, including Park units. Finally, the Parking Shuttle Loop links the numerous parking facilities to Park units and important sites in Morristown via connection to the ATS at the main 'transportation hub,' thus allowing residents and visitors to park their vehicle and experience the units of the Park and Morristown on an ATS shuttle. Each loop is described in the summaries that follow.

3.1.1 Jockey Hollow Interpretive Loops

Two routes are proposed for the Jockey Hollow Encampment Area (see Figure 6). These routes would use a tram-type vehicle and focus on improving the visitor experience at Jockey Hollow. Both routes would begin at the Jockey Hollow Visitor Center. The shorter route would pass by the Wick House and stop at the Pennsylvania Line (Soldiers' Huts). It would then proceed on Grand Parade Road to a stop at the New York Brigade Comfort Station. This route is 2.8 miles in length. The longer route, 3.9 miles, would also begin at the Jockey Hollow Visitor Center, stop at the Wick House and Pennsylvania Lin, but would proceed on Sugar Loaf Road, past the entrance to Lewis Morris Park, and on to the New York Brigade Comfort Station by way of Jockey Hollow Road. Further discussion about the operating season for these loops is required (e.g. operating season may be year-round or May through September). In this study, we assume an operating season of 360 days.

The Jockey Hollow Interpretive Loops would provide benefits other than interpretation, including safety and air pollution reduction due to a decrease in cars traveling on the Park roads. These routes, alone, would not address the goals to connect to downtown transit opportunities or enhance general tourism and economic development in Morristown and Morris County. Nor would either of these alternatives help encourage visits to the Park's multiple units. One of these alternatives could operate in addition to the more comprehensive alternatives presented in Section 3.1.2.

Volpe National Transportation Systems Center

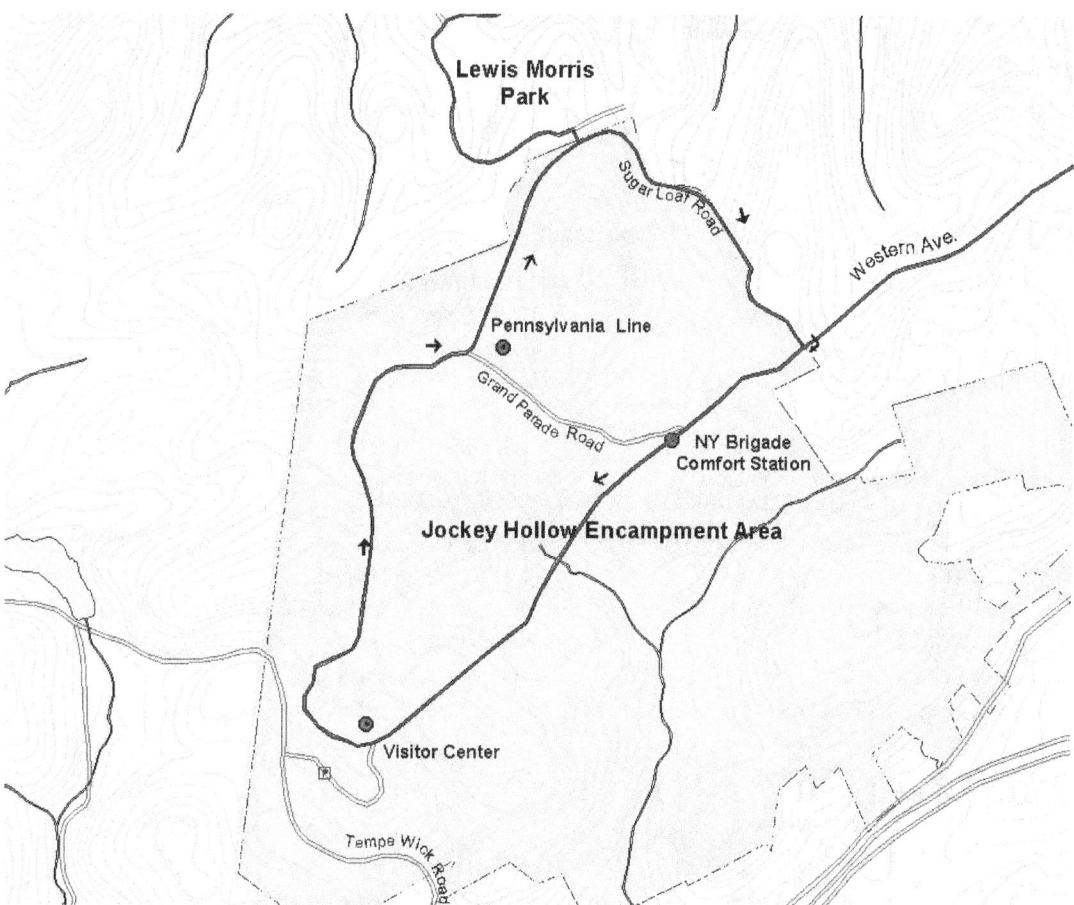

Figure 7. Jockey Holley Interpretive Loops

3.1.2 Town-wide Loops
A second set of alternatives links significant employment centers, retail areas, and cultural and Historical sites in Morristown. This study offers two circuits under this alternative: the "Park Circuit" and the "Local Circuit." The Park Circuit would connect three of the four Park units (Jockey Hollow Visitor Center, Fort Nonsense, and Washington Headquarters) to sites in Morristown; whereas, the Local Circuit would not include any Park units, but instead connects other sites forming an integrated network.

The Park Circuit would operate a "Summer" and "Winter" Route. The routes would include the following stops:

Park Circuit - Summer Route	Park Circuit - Winter Route
Frelinguysen Arboretum	Frelinguysen Arboretum
Westin Hotel	Westin Hotel
Acorn Hall	Acorn Hall
Washington Headquarters	Washington Headquarters
Morristown Train Station	Morristown Train Station
South Street Shopping Area	Morristown Green
Morristown Green	Headquarters Plaza Hotel
Headquarters Plaza Hotel	Fort Nonsense
Fort Nonsense	New York Brigade
New York Brigade Comfort Station	Jockey Hollow Visitor
Jockey Hollow Visitor Center	Pennsylvania Line
Pennsylvania Line	Fort Nonsense
Lewis Morris Park	Morristown Green
Fosterfields	Headquarters Plaza Hotel
Burnham Park	Morristown Train Station
Fort Nonsense	Washington Headquarters
Morristown Green	Frelinguysen Arboretum
Headquarters Plaza Hotel	
Morristown Train Station	
Washington Headquarters	
Frelinguysen Arboretum	

The summer route (18.7[11] miles for a complete circuit) would include all of the Park units except the New Jersey Brigade Encampment Area, three major recreation / cultural sites, two of the major hotels (Headquarters Plaza Hotel and Westin Hotel), two other important cultural attractions in Morristown, as well as downtown shopping and restaurants. It could be operated alone or in conjunction with the Local Circuit, or one of the Jockey Hollow Interpretive Loop alternatives. The Winter Route (17 miles for a complete circuit) would be the same as the Summer Route, but without stops at Lewis Morris Park, Fosterfields, and Burnham Park.

The Local Circuit (7.9[12] miles for a complete circuit) would connect the Morristown Hospital, Morristown Green, and some of the major employment and shopping centers in the downtown area and along Mount Kemble Avenue. The Local Circuit could be combined with the Park Circuit, and would offer attractive partnership opportunities with other organizations.

---

[11] Based on comments received during a meeting with local stakeholders on October 3, 2001, this route was changed slightly to include the South Street Shopping Area after the Morristown Train Station and before the Morristown Green. Therefore, the route's distance of 18.7 is only an estimate.

[12] Based on comments received during a meeting with local stakeholders on October 3, 2001, this route was changed slightly to include the South Street Shopping Area after the Morristown Train Station and before the Morristown Green. Therefore, the route's distance of 7.9 is only an estimate.

Volpe National Transportation Systems Center

It would include the following stops:

<u>Local Circuit</u>

Morristown Train Station
South Street Shopping Area
Morristown Green
Best Western Hotel
Morristown Hospital
South Street Shopping Area
Morristown Green

Headquarters Plaza Hotel
Morristown Rehabilitation Hospital
AT&T Corporate Headquarters
Morristown Green
Headquarters Plaza Hotel
Morristown Train Station

The map shows the two routes and all of the proposed stops. Please note that "Route 1" refers to the Park Circuit and "Route 2" refers to the Local Circuit.

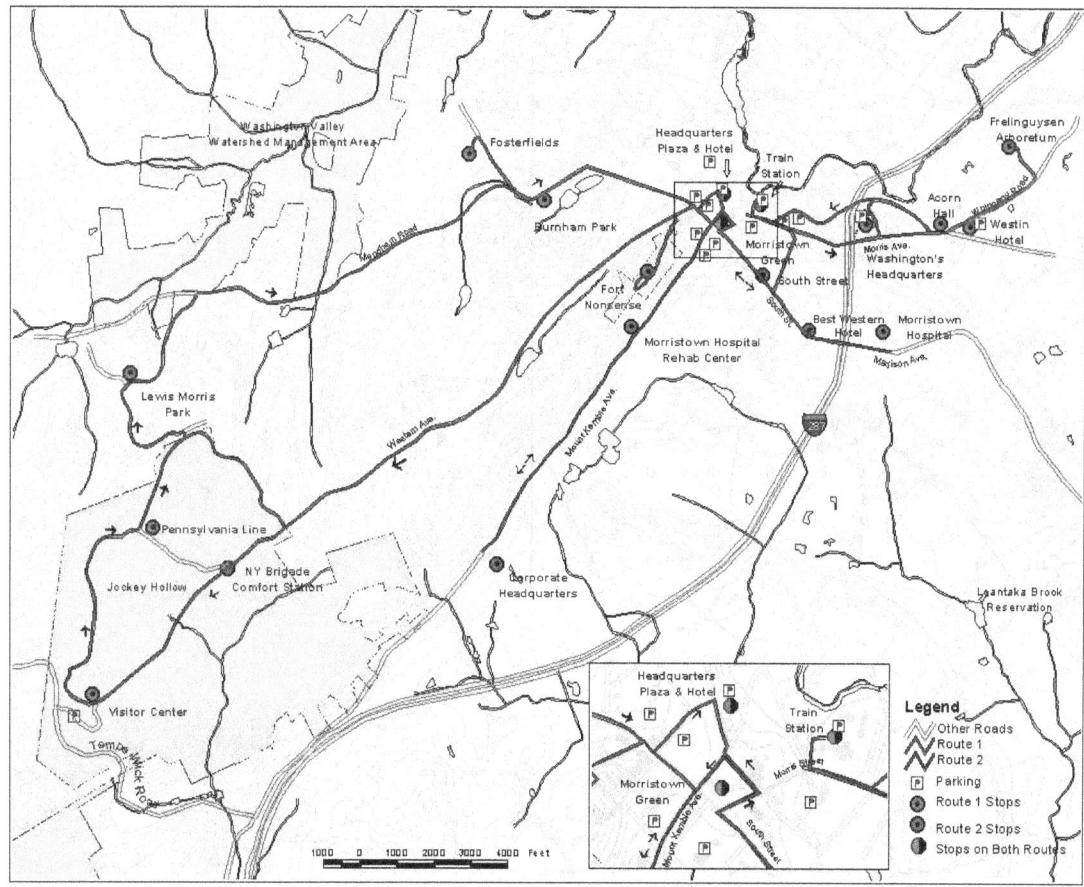

Figure 8. Town-wide Loop

Recommendations from TransOptions[13] and Morristown Partnership[14], based on a high concentration of retail and commercial establishments, are to include ATS stops at the intersection of

---

[13] Judy Maltese and Donald Watt of TransOptions kindly provided recommendations.
[14] Paul Miller of Morristown Partnership kindly provided recommendations.

Volpe National Transportation Systems Center

Western Avenue and Washington Street and possibly at Pete's Restaurant located at 121 Morris Avenue across from the train station for the Park and Local Circuits. They also recommended 83 South Street for the ATS stop on South Street (Local Circuit).

3.1.3 Parking Shuttle Loop

The last proposed loop would connect the designated 'Intercept' parking facilities within Morristown to the main 'transportation hub' for the ATS. The parking shuttle loop connects various parking facilities within the center of Morristown that are recommended to be designated as 'Intercept' parking facilities (see Section 2.6). The Parking Shuttle Loop would collect and distribute residents and visitors to and from these facilities and bring them to the main 'transportation hub' for access to the ATS. At this point, we do not have enough information to identify ATS stop locations.

3.1.4 Morristown Green – Main Transportation Hub

The two Town-wide Loops share several common stops—Morristown Green, Morristown Train Station, and the Headquarters Plaza Hotel. Passengers interchanging between the two town-wide loops would occur at these common access points. The Morristown Green would serve as the main 'transportation hub.' It is an ideal focal point and an important Historical feature. General Washington was quartered in Jacob's Tavern on the Morristown Green during the winter of 1777. The lovely setting of the Morristown Green also would alleviate the inconvenience of passenger waiting time. Transit amenities, such as an attractive bus shelter(s) could be added to improve the experience of waiting for the bus. The Morristown Green is within close walking distance of numerous parking areas, allowing visitors to park in one of these areas and use the ATS as their way of exploring the town and Park. It is a short walk to the Morristown Train Station, the Headquarters Plaza Hotel, shopping, and restaurants. In addition, one can begin the Historical Morristown Walking Tour from the Morristown Green. For the ATS Parking Shuttle Loop circuits envisioned, approximately 200 feet are needed to site two curbside bus bays that would permit independent entry and exit at seven miles per hour[15]. This would require the removal and possible mitigation of parking spaces. Furthermore, the Morristown Green is a privately owned site and the owners would have to agree to allow such use. Because of the one-way traffic patterns on the street adjacent to the Morristown Green, and the fact that transit vehicles have right-side doors only, the ATS loading and unloading zone would actually be situated along the curbs opposite the Morristown Green.

Another possible location for a 'transportation hub' would be the Morristown Train Station. The Morristown Train Station is an important stop on both loops. It lacks some of the aesthetic appeal of the Morristown Green and would take riders further away from shopping and restaurants, but it makes an easy multi-modal connector for commuters and tourists. The Jockey Hollow Visitors Center is a common point for the Jockey Hollow interpretive loop and the town-wide park circuit.

3.1.5 Connections to Morristown Hotels

The proposed Park and Local Circuits stop at Headquarters Plaza Hotel. In addition, the Park Circuit would stop at the Westin Hotel; and, the Local Circuit would stop at the Best Western Hotel and near the proposed Inn at Vail Mansion on South Street.

---

[15] The minimum design requirements for an on-street bus berth are L + 25 meters, where L is the length of the design vehicle. See G. A. Giannopoulos, Bus Planning and Operation in Urban Areas, 1989.

Volpe National Transportation Systems Center

A direct tie-in of the ATS to the hotels is critical for several reasons: (1) the hotels could be a prime source of visitors (currently 515 total rooms[16]) and potential generators of patronage for the ATS; (2) it allows shared use of the hotels' parking, site drop-off and loading zones, and lobby/waiting room amenities for the convenience of ATS passengers; (3) it permits convenient access to and interchange among the ATS circuits, with each circuit acting as a feeder of patrons to the other; and (4) it facilitates the possibility of equitable cost-sharing among the private and public partners. Any of the hotels could make direct contributions as corporate sponsors, or perhaps an innovative financing plan can be implemented, such as a room occupancy surcharge with a free pass to the ATS for the duration of a visitor's occupancy, which is currently being explored.

3.2 ATS Operating Characteristics

This section provides a description of the proposed ATS configuration options with tables that present the operating parameters and performance metrics for each option. Operating parameter definitions are in Appendix B. Explanations for calculating the cycle time and minimum fleet size are presented in Appendix C.

A number of assumptions about the ATS operating characteristics were made in order to calibrate operating parameters, proximate vehicle requirements, and performance metrics for each route. All assumptions are subject to reconsideration by the Park. The proposed routes are assumed to operate 360 days a year; however, the Park may prefer to operate some or all of the routes from May through September. The span of operating service is assumed to be from 8:30 AM to 5:00 PM; however, the service could begin earlier or later and end later, particularly if the service is in partnership with local stakeholders. In addition, the proposed routes assume that the headway does not exceed 30 minutes. This headway ensures that no passenger waits longer than 30 minutes for a vehicle.

Jockey Hollow Interpretative Loops

As described in Section 3.1.1, the actual routing of a Jockey Hollow Interpretative Loop could take one of two variants in route design: via Grand Parade or via Sugar Loaf Road. Based on a discussion with NPS staff[17], the intent of establishing a Jockey Hollow interpretative loop is to provide more than a method of mobility to access units within Jockey Hollow. While the loop would connect with important trailheads and other interpretive sites within Jockey Hollow for further exploration and enjoyment by Visitors, the intent is also to provide an orientation to Jockey Hollow via a non-intrusive interpretative program offered on the vehicle. The nature of the Jockey Hollow interpretative loop lends itself quite well to a tram-like vehicle (travel is solely within the confines of Jockey Hollow on park-owned roads, and speeds are limited to a relatively slow 20-25 mph). This would be our recommendation, except that we would also suggest acquisition of a trailer unit[18] to be used during peak Visitor loads. Assuming a minimal design for the loop consisting of 1 tram (with trailer unit, if necessary), the operational characteristics, given the functional characteristics of this ATS Jockey Hollow Interpretative Loop, are given below in Tables 6 and 7.

---

[16] The opening of the Inn at Vail Mansion by 2003, will add 101 rooms.
[17] Discussion with Brian Aviles, Boston Support Office for Northeast Region, National Park Service, General Management Plan (GMP) team captain.
[18] Non-powered unit that easily connects to the powered tram. The trailer increases the passenger capacity of the tram by approximately 20-25 passengers.

Volpe National Transportation Systems Center

Table 6. Operating Parameters - Jockey Hollow Interpretative Loop

Name	Value	Source
Travel Time	8.4/11.7 minutes	Calculated based on 20 mph, and route length for the two variants in route design
Dwell Time (Allowable Interpretative Time	15 minutes	Maximum allowable based on constraint of a minimal system design consisting of 1 ATS vehicle
Terminal Layover	5 minutes	Reasonable assumption
Headway	30 minutes	Assumed operating policy
Stopping Time Penalty	10 seconds	Calculated based on vehicle speed and acceleration/deceleration
Station Stops	3	Calculated from route design layout and objectives for the interpretative program.
Span of Service	8:30 AM – 5:30 PM	Assumed operating policy, with constant service throughout the day.
Operating Season	360 days	Assumed operating season.

Table 7. Performance Metrics - Jockey Hollow Interpretative Loop

Performance Metric	Value	Source
Cycle Time	30 minutes	Calculated, equation 1
Fleet Size	1	Calculated, equation 2
Vehicle Hours Traveled	3,240 per annum	Calculated[19]
Vehicle Miles Traveled	50.4/70.2 per day 18,144-25,272 per annum	Calculated[20]
Passenger Service Interval at Stops	30 minutes	Assumed operating policy
Vehicle Trips	18 per day	Calculated[21]

Town-wide Loop - Park Circuit

While precise estimates of station-to-station passenger demand are difficult to estimate, general considerations in the planning and design of the Park Circuit do suggest a plausible ridership scenario that permits an estimate of the aggregate dwell time needed to compute the cycle time. This is possible despite not knowing precise numbers of passengers boarding and alighting at the individual stops along the Park Circuit.

---

[19] Calculated as: [N_{peak}* 4 hours + $N_{off\text{-}peak}$* 5 hours] * 360 days per annum
[20] Calculated as: 2 vehicle trips per hour * 2.8 (3.9) miles per trip * 9 operating hours; [50.4 (70.2) miles per day * 360 days of service per year].
[21] Calculated as: 60/h = 2 vehicle trips per hour *9 operating hours per day.

Volpe National Transportation Systems Center

The Park Circuit links three of the four discrete Park units. In the summer operating season (Memorial Day through Labor Day), the Park Circuit route would also serve Lewis Morris Park, Burnham Park and Fosterfields via Mendham Road. The winter operating season would route the ATS vehicles on the return trip from Jockey Hollow via Western Avenue, and the latter three local recreational and cultural sites would not be served. The ATS concept plan as delineated in this study, envisions private vehicle access via the main arterials serving Morristown to a series of 'intercept' parking facilities that ring the Morristown CBD. Connection to the ATS would be via well-signed pedestrian pathways to the main 'transportation hub' at the Morristown Green or at the Morristown Train Station, or connection via an 'intercept' parking shuttle loop. The ATS Park Circuit also has a direct tie into two of the primary hotels (Headquarters Plaza Hotel and Westin Hotel). The Morristown Green, Morristown Train Station, and the two hotels serve as 'common access points' to the ATS, thus the primary passenger origination and termination points, and where transfers can be made to other routes in the ATS that would also converge at these 'common access points.' Therefore, one can construct a plausible ridership scenario based on the following assumptions:

- The great majority of passengers originate and terminate at the 'common access points' (i.e., Morristown Green, Morristown Train Station, Headquarters Plaza Hotel, and Westin Hotel), with intermediate stops at the Park.
- Conversely, a relatively small number of passengers originate and terminate at the Park units and/or other sites served by the route.
- Visitation duration at each of the Park units exceeds the headway interval of the service; therefore at each of the Park units there is a full interchange of passengers on board the ATS vehicle. All passengers on-board alight from the current vehicle run, and waiting passengers board from an earlier vehicle run.
- ATS vehicles run full during peak hours between Washington Headquarters and the Jockey Hollow Visitor Center, and at 60 percent of ATS vehicle capacity over the same segment during the off-peak hours.
- Marginal alighting time per passenger is two seconds, and marginal boarding time per passenger is four seconds.

Table 8 presents values of operating parameters that have been used, on the basis of which we have calculated and presented in Table 9 the *cycle time*, the minimal fleet size (i.e., number of ATS vehicles) needed to operate the ATS Park Circuit, and the other performance metrics. Tables 10 and 11 provide corresponding information for the winter routing of the Park Circuit.

Table 8: Operating Parameters - Park Circuit (Summer Route)

Operating Parameter	Value: Peak	Off-Peak	Source
Travel Time	53 min	46.2 min	Estimated adjustment to winter routing which was measured, based on sample vehicle runs
Dwell Time	15 min	8.4 min	Calculated, equation 3
Terminal Layover	5 min	5 min	Reasonable assumption
Headway	30 min	30 min	Assumed operating policy

Volpe National Transportation Systems Center

Operating Parameter	Value: Peak Off-Peak	Source
Stopping Time Penalty	8 sec 10 sec	Calculated, based on reasonable peak and off-peak running speeds, and ATS vehicle acceleration and deceleration rates[22]
Passenger Demand Rate	120 pass/hr 60 pass/hr	Reasonable (perhaps optimistic) assumption
Station Stops	20 20	Calculated from Route design layout
Service Processing Rate	20 events/min 20 events/min	Calculated, based on average of marginal alighting and boarding time
Capacity	30 pass 18 pass	Maximum passenger load on ATS vehicle
Span of Service	8:30AM-10:30AM 10:30AM-3:30PM 3:30PM-5:30PM	Assumed operating policy
Operating Season	99 days	Assumed operating season from Memorial Day to Labor Day.

Table 9. Performance Metrics - Park Circuit (Summer Route)

Performance Metric	Value: Peak Off-Peak	Source
Cycle Time	75.7 min 62.9 min	Calculated, equation 1
Fleet Size	3 vehicles 3 vehicles	Calculated, equation 2
Vehicle Hours Traveled	2,673 per annum	Calculated[23]
Vehicle Miles Traveled	149.6 per day 187 per day 33,323 per annum	Calculated[24]
Passenger Service Interval at Stops	30 min 30 min	Assumed operating policy
Vehicle Trips	8 per day 10 per day	Calculated[25]
Daily Ridership	480 pass 300 pass	Calculated[26]
Passengers per ATS Vehicle Trip	60 pass 30 pass	Calculated[27]
Maximum Bi-directional Passenger Flow Capacity of ATS at Park Unit Stops	120 pass/hr 120 pass/hr	Calculated[28]

---

[22] Calculation based on $V/2[1/a + 1/b]$, with V being running speed, and a, b acceleration and deceleration rates respectively.
[23] Calculated as: $[N_{peak} * 4 \text{ hours} + N_{off\text{-}peak} * 5 \text{ hours}] * 99$ days per annum
[24] Calculated as: 2 vehicle trips per hour * 18.7 miles per trip * 4 peak hours; 2 vehicle trips per hour * 18.7 miles per trip * 5 off-peak hours; [149.6 peak hour miles + 187 off-peak hour miles] * 99 days of service per year.
[25] Calculated as: 60/h = 2 vehicle trips per hour * 4 peak hours per day; 60/h = 2 vehicle trips per hour * 5 off-peak hours per day.
[26] Calculated as: $p_{peak} * 4$ peak hours; $p_{off\text{-}peak} * 5$ off-peak hours
[27] Calculated as: 480 daily peak hour passengers/ 8 peak-hour vehicle trips; 300 daily off-peak passengers/ 10 off-peak hour vehicle trips.
[28] Calculated as: 2 vehicle trips per hour * c (ATS vehicle capacity or maximum load) for drop-off + 2 vehicle trips per hour * c for pick-up.

Volpe National Transportation Systems Center

Table 10. Operating Parameters - Park Circuit (Winter Route)

Operating Parameter	Value: Peak Off-Peak	Source
Travel Time	49.4 min 42.6 min	Measured, based on sample vehicle runs
Dwell Time	15 min 8.4 min	Calculated, equation 3
Terminal Layover	5 min 5 min	Reasonable assumption
Headway	30 min 30 min	Assumed operating policy
Stopping Time Penalty	8 sec 10 sec	Calculated, based on reasonable peak and off-peak running speeds, and ATS vehicle acceleration and deceleration rates[29]
Passenger Demand Rate	120 pass/hr 60 pass/hr	Reasonable (perhaps optimistic) assumption
Station Stops	17 17	Calculated from Route design layout
Service Processing Rate	20 events/min 20 events/min	Calculated, based on average of marginal alighting and boarding time
Capacity	30 pass 18 pass	Maximum passenger load on ATS vehicle
Span of Service	8:30AM-10:30AM 10:30AM-3:30PM 3:30PM-5:30PM	Assumed operating policy
Operating Season	261 days	Assumed operating season from Labor Day to Memorial Day.

Table 11. Performance Metrics - Park Circuit (Winter Route)

Performance Metric	Value: Peak Off-Peak	Source
Cycle Time	71.8 min 59 min	Calculated, equation 1
Fleet Size	3 vehicles 2 vehicles	Calculated, equation 2
Vehicle Hours Traveled	5,742 per annum	Calculated[30]
Vehicle Miles Traveled	140.8 per day 176 per day 82,685 per annum	Calculated[31]
Passenger Service Interval at Stops	30 min 30 min	Assumed operating policy
Vehicle Trips	8 per day 10 per day	Calculated[32]
Daily Ridership	480 pass 300 pass	Calculated[33]
Passengers per ATS Vehicle Trip	60 pass 30 pass	Calculated[34]

---

[29] Calculation based on $V/2[1/a + 1/b]$, with V being running speed, and a, b acceleration and deceleration rates respectively.
[30] Calculated as: $[N_{peak}* 4 \text{ hours} + N_{off-peak}* 5 \text{ hours}] * 261$ days per annum
[31] Calculated as: 2 vehicle trips per hour * 17.6 miles per trip * 4 peak hours; 2 vehicle trips per hour * 17.6 miles per trip * 5 off-peak hours; [140.8 peak hour miles + 176 off-peak hour miles] * 261 days of service per year.
[32] Calculated as: 60/h = 2 vehicle trips per hour * 4 peak hours per day; 60/h = 2 vehicle trips per hour * 5 off-peak hours per day.
[33] Calculated as: p_{peak} * 4 peak hours; $p_{off-peak}$ * 5 off-peak hours

Volpe National Transportation Systems Center

Performance Metric	Value: Peak Off-Peak	Source
Maximum Bi-directional Passenger Flow Capacity of ATS at Park Unit Stops	120 pass/hr 120 pass/hr	Calculated[35]

Table 12 provides a comparison of the visitation levels in Table 4 with the maximum passenger flow capacity[36] of an initial design for the ATS. The maximum passenger flow capacity indicates what percentage of the estimated visitors could be serviced by an ATS, considering the number of ATS vehicles per hour, capacity of an ATS vehicle, and the number of hours the ATS is operating. For example, 70 percent of the visitors to Tempe Wick between the months of May and October could be serviced by an ATS.

Table 12. ATS passenger flow capacity as percent of Average Day Visitation

Year	Tempe Wick	Western Ave Gate	Fort Nonsense	Cross Estate	Washington Headquarter
3-year average, May-Oct	70	79	100+	100+	100+
3-year average, Nov-April	100+	100+	100+	100+	100+

Town-wide Loop – Local Circuit

The intent of the ATS Local Circuit is to serve a variety of retail and business activity centers beyond local recreational, Historical and cultural sites (e.g., the retail/business center along South Street, and the major hospitals and AT&T Corporate Center). It is expected that the ATS Local Circuit would be operated in conjunction with the ATS Park Circuit, allowing for good connectivity between the Park units and local employment/commercial centers within Morristown. Passenger interchange between the two routes would take place at the 'common access points'.

Given the characteristics of this route design, one can construct a plausible ridership scenario based on the following assumptions:

- The pattern of passenger origination and termination is more diffuse across the set of stops.
- Commuters are a sizeable portion of the expected ridership, with the major employment center at the AT&T Corporate Headquarters as the maximum load point for the route (alighting in the AM; boarding in the PM).
- ATS Vehicles run full in the peak to AT&T Corporate Headquarters, with 50 percent of the on-board passengers alighting and boarding in the AM and PM peak respectively.
- Marginal alighting time per passenger is two seconds, and marginal boarding time per passenger is four seconds.

---

[34] Calculated as: 480 daily peak hour passengers/ 8 peak-hour vehicle trips; 300 daily off-peak passengers/ 10 off-peak hour vehicle trips.
[35] Calculated as: 2 vehicle trips per hour * c (ATS vehicle capacity or maximum load) for drop-off + 2 vehicle trips per hour * c for pick-up.
[36] Calculated as ATS vehicles per hour * capacity of an ATS vehicle * span of service; i.e., $2*c*9 = 60*9 = 540$ passengers per day that can be delivered to Park Units

Volpe National Transportation Systems Center

The Local Circuit's operating parameters and performance metrics are presented in Tables 13 and 14.

Table 13. Operating Parameters - Local Circuit

Operating Parameter	Value: Peak Off-Peak	Source
Travel Time	31 min 25.1 min	Estimated adjustment to measured value, based on sample vehicle runs on an earlier route design
Dwell Time	6.75 min 6 min	Calculated, equation (4a), (4b)
Terminal Layover	5 min 5 min	Reasonable assumption
Headway	30 min 30 min	Assumed operating policy
Stopping Time Penalty	8 sec 10 sec	Calculated, based on reasonable peak and off-peak running speeds, and ATS vehicle acceleration and deceleration rates[37]
Passenger Demand Rate	120 pass/hr 60 pass/hr	Reasonable (perhaps optimistic) assumption
Station Stops	11 11	Calculated from Route design layout
Service Processing Rate	20 events/min 20 events/min	Calculated, based on average of marginal alighting and boarding time
Capacity	30 pass 18 pass	Maximum passenger load on ATS vehicle
Span of Service	8:30AM-10:30AM 3:30PM-5:30PM 10:30AM-3:30PM	Assumed operating policy
Operating Season	360 days	Assumed operating season.

Table 14. Performance Metrics - ATS Local Circuit

Performance Metric	Value: Peak Off-Peak	Source
Cycle Time	44.2 min 37.9 min	Calculated, equation 1
Fleet Size	2 vehicles 2 vehicles	Calculated, equation 2
Vehicle Hours Traveled	6,480 per annum	Calculated[38]
Vehicle Miles Traveled	63.0 per day 78.8 per day 51,048 per annum	Calculated[39]
Passenger Service Interval at Stops	30 min 30 min	Assumed operating policy
Vehicle Trips	8 per day 10 per day	Calculated[40]

[37] Calculation based on $V/2[1/a + 1/b]$, with V being running speed, and a, b acceleration and deceleration rates respectively.
[38] Calculated as: $[N_{peak} * 4 \text{ hours} + N_{off-peak} * 5 \text{ hours}] * 360$ days per annum
[39] Calculated as: 2 vehicle trips per hour * 7.88 miles per trip * 4 peak hours; 2 vehicle trips per hour * 7.88 miles per trip * 5 off-peak hours; [63.0 peak hour miles + 78.8 off-peak hour miles] * 360 days of service per year.
[40] Calculated as: $60/h$ = 2 vehicle trips per hour * 4 peak hours per day; $60/h$ = 2 vehicle trips per hour * 5 off-peak hours per day.

Volpe National Transportation Systems Center

Performance Metric	Value: Peak Off-Peak	Source
Daily Ridership	480 pass 300 pass	Calculated[41]
Passengers per ATS Vehicle Trip	60 pass 30 pass	Calculated[42]

Intercept Parking Circuit

Depending upon which of several potential parking facilities that ring the center of Morristown are designated as 'intercept' parking facilities for the ATS, an ATS Intercept Parking Circuit shuttle service may also be operated. The function of this shuttle loop would be to collect and distribute visitors between these parking facilities and the main 'transportation hub' for the ATS. If the designated facilities are in good proximity to the main 'transportation hub' or other 'common access points' for the ATS (i.e., where the systems' routes converge), the existing pedestrian pathway system would be used to direct visitors to the ATS. Good way-finding signage[43] would be established along the major arterials to direct both residents and visitors to the 'intercept' parking facilities. Likewise, a signage system would be implemented to direct residents and visitors from the 'intercept' parking facilities to the ATS main 'transportation hub' for access to the system. This signage could be integrated with the *Exterior Wayfinding Sign Program*[44], which was proposed for Morristown's Special Improvement District. Until further information is developed in conjunction with the local stakeholders, however, no operational analysis similar to the above ATS routes can be made.

3.3   Comparison of Transportation Alternatives

The NPS' *Choose By Advantage* method provides a helpful framework to assess the benefits of the routes. Table 15 provides an analysis of individual routes. It is important to note, however, that more than one of these loops could be implemented. Some routes, such as the Parking Shuttle Loop, would have minimal benefit to the Park if operated alone. Accompanying each factor, are brief comments describing how an ATS will satisfy the factor. For each factor, the route is assessed, using a grading system of (H)igh, (M)edium, and (L)ow.

Table 15. Choose By Advantage

Factor	Jockey Hollow Loop	Town-wide (Park)	Town-wide (Town)	Parking Shuttle Loop
Prevent Loss of Resources • Operation of an ATS will reduce use of private vehicles in and around the Park resulting in improved air quality and decreased traffic congestion.	M	H	M	M
Maintain or Improve the Condition of Resources • An ATS will result in greater visitation to the Park	M	H	L	L

---

[41] Calculated as: p_{peak} * 4 peak hours; $p_{off-peak}$ * 5 off-peak hours
[42] Calculated as: 480 daily peak hour passengers/ 8 peak-hour vehicle trips; 300 daily off-peak passengers/ 10 off-peak hour vehicle trips.
[43] An ATS logo symbol or icon, in conjunction with the international symbol for parking (P) would be sited at all strategic decision points for motorists along all the major arterials that converge on the center of Morristown.
[44] Exterior Wayfinding Sign Program developed by Desman Associates for the Morristown Special Improvement District, March 26, 2001.

Volpe National Transportation Systems Center

Factor	Jockey Hollow Loop	Town-wide (Park)	Town-wide (Town)	Parking Shuttle Loop
units, which will create a regular NPS presence in these units, reducing the potential for criminal activities including archeological theft.				
Provide Visitor Services and Educational and Recreational Services • Operation of an ATS will connect Park units and local cultural sites. • An ATS will improve visitors' experience by relieving them of driving unfamiliar and congested roads. • The ATS will be an interpretive and learning vehicle. • The ATS will provide connections between trailheads and other transportation nodes.	M	H	L	L
Protect Public Health, Safety, and Welfare • An ATS will lessen the exposure of Park visitors, often families with children, to hazardous and confusing driving conditions. • An ATS will reduce private vehicle usage, thus improve air quality.	M	H	M	M
Improve Operational Efficiency and Sustainability • The ATS will enable Park employees to commute or circulate between Park units in place of private or government vehicles. • The ATS will even-out visitation among Park units, thus enabling the Park staff to program activities at these units more regularly.	L	H	L	L
Protect Employee Health, Safety, and Welfare • An ATS will enable Park staff to commute or circulate between Park units in place of private or government vehicles, reducing stress and exposure to hazardous driving conditions.	L	H	L	L
Provide Other Advantages to the NPS • An ATS, developed in partnership with regional stakeholders, presents the NPS as an approachable, creative organization engaged with local citizens in improving the quality of life and of the parks. • A multi-agency ATS will allow all stakeholders to address regional issues beyond the scope of any one agency.	L	H	H	H

Volpe National Transportation Systems Center

3.4 Funding Requirements

Vehicle capital and operating and maintenance costs for each of the proposed ATS options are presented in Table 16.

Table 16. Vehicle Capital and Operating and Maintenance Costs

	Jockey Hollow Interpretive Loop	Town-wide Loop			Parking Shuttle Loop	Spare Vehicles
	Short & Long Circuits	*Park Circuit*		*Local Circuit*		
		Winter	Summer			
Vehicle requirement	1	3	3	2	2	2
Vehicle capital cost	250,000	750,000	750,000	500,000	500,000	500,000
Annual Operations and Maintenance Cost	162,000	287,100	133,650	324,000	TBD	

An upper-bound amount of 250,000 dollars per vehicle was used to determine the Vehicle Capital Cost. Vehicle prices range from 130,000 (e.g. Trolley Enterprise diesel trolley) to 250,000 (Chance Coach diesel trolley) dollars. It is important to note that if the vehicles were acquired by a public agency (e.g. Morristown Parking Authority), the Federal Transit Agency (FTA) could pay for 80 percent of the vehicle acquisition costs. Other capital costs have not yet been determined. The annual operations and maintenance cost is calculated by multiplying hourly operating and maintenance cost times annual vehicle hours traveled. An upper-bound figure of 50 dollars an hour was estimated for operations and maintenance costs. No estimates were calculated for the parking shuttle loop due to a lack of specificity about the Parking Shuttle Loop at this time.

3.5 Vehicle Options

In order for the new system to be successfully initiated and accepted as a viable means of accessing the Park and other Morristown sites, vehicles procured need to be reliable, comfortable, and easily recognizable. At the meeting with local stakeholders on October 3, 2001, participants voiced strong interest in using a distinctive looking vehicle, such as a trolley, rather than a standard bus. While it is not the intent to discuss vehicle options in great depth, it is important to identify attractive features to look for in procuring vehicles. We recommend that the Town-wide and Parking Shuttle Loops use vehicles with tight turning radii. The tight turning radius is critical for maneuvering around Fort Nonsense[45]. Vehicles must be Americans with Disabilities Act (ADA) accessible. Other characteristics of a good vehicle include:

- High scores in all of the areas of the 12-year Altoona Test.
- Securement for wheelchairs.
- Ramp extension rather than a lift.
- Easy accessibility for boarding and alighting the bus.
- Wide doors and aisles that allow for faster boarding.
- Large windows, allowing for greater visibility both for the driver and visitors.
- Superior construction for increased strength and a longer life span.

---

[45] The minimum turning radius needed for Fort Nonsense is not known at this time because no measurements were taken.

Volpe National Transportation Systems Center

- Excellent passenger and driver comfort.
- Flexibility in seating configuration.

The tram-vehicle proposed for the Jockey Hollow Interpretive Loop could be a relatively shorter vehicle (e.g. 24 feet) with good power to weight ratio in order to pull a non-powered trailer. Figure 9 is one example of this type of vehicle. Based on local stakeholders' preference to have a distinctive-looking vehicle for the Town-wide and Parking Shuttle Loops, we have included some examples of trolley replica buses (Figures 10 – 14). Please note that this study presents only a few of the manufactures available. The Volpe Center does not endorse any specific company.

Figure 9. Specialty Vehicles 5000 Series

Figure 10. EV22T Manufactured by EVI (E-bus)Electric

Figure 11. Chance Coach American Heritage Streetcar, Diesel and CNG options

Figure 12. DuponTrolley, Diesel

Figure 13. Trolley Enterprises, Electric, Hybrid, and Propane Options

Figure 14. Holland Bus Company, Diesel

4. SYSTEM MANAGEMENT

The ATS route options, depending on which is chosen, allow planning and operations to proceed separately by the Park and Morristown or Morris County. The Park needs to decide whether they want to take on the operations and maintenance of a transit system, contract for the ATS, or partner with a local government agency or public/private entity. This section presents four management options, including:

- Option 1 - Morristown NHP purchases the vehicles and hires permanent or term employees as drivers
- Option 2 - Contracting to a third party to provide vehicles, drivers, and maintenance
- Option 3 - NPS buys the equipment, then obtains drivers and maintenance through a service contract(s)
- Option 4 - Partnering with a local government agency or a public-private organization

Each option has benefits and risks associated with it. Table 17 provides a summary of the capital costs, operating costs, staffing requirements, and new facilities needed for the Park Circuit (summer route), as an example. A detailed description of each system management option is provided in the text that follows the tables. This study does not include a Choose By Advantage analysis for the management options. Further study and collaboration with the potential stakeholders is necessary to assess the management options.

Table 17. Costs of Management Options

	Option 1	Option 2	Option 3	Option 4
Capital Costs	$750,000	0	$750,000	$750,000
Annual Operating & Maintenance Costs	$133,658	$525,000[46]	$525,000	$133,650
Park Staffing Requirements	$312,000 for 4 NPS Drivers	None	None	None
New NPS Facilities Needed	NPS Storage for Trolleys/Buses at Park	None	None	None

(1) Morristown NHP purchases the vehicles and hires permanent or term employees as drivers

Option 1 envisions the Park responsible for the entire cost and effort of operating and maintaining the ATS. This option could be appropriate for those route options serving the Park units: Town-Wide Park Circuits (Summer and Winter) and the Jockey Hollow Interpretive Loops. The staffing model is similar to how Lowell NHP operates their trolley and canal boats.

Under this model the Park's GMP would reflect an increase in permanent full time employee (FTE) and expanded vehicle storage at the Jockey Hollow utility area. Hiring permanent or term

---

[46] Using Adams NHP figure of $175,000 per vehicle and driver, the Park Circuit (summer route) operating and maintenance costs for Options 2 and 3 would be $525,000.

Volpe National Transportation Systems Center

employees, with commercial licenses, to operate the vehicles would cost approximately 38 dollars per hour or 78,000 dollars annually (base salary plus benefits). For the Park Circuit (summer), as an example, the Park would need four drivers (three to run the system and one for emergency backup). The cost to the Park for four drivers would be approximately 312,000 dollars. Fuel is estimated to be about 49,000 dollars per year (i.e. 2.00 dollars a gallon of diesel times 121,176 VMT/5 miles a gallon). Oil changes can be contracted out to a "Jiffy Lube" type service estimated for the three vehicles at 1,500 dollars. Cleaning services can also be contracted also estimated at an additional 1,500 dollars per annum. The vehicles from the General Services Administration schedule have warranties for three years and assume low maintenance in the beginning of the lifecycle, but can be estimated conservatively at 1,000 dollars per vehicle per year for a total of 3,000 dollars. Total fuel and maintenance costs can then be estimated at 55,000 dollars. Insurance is not required for vehicles operated by the Federal government even those that have "non-Federal" passengers. The costs therefore do not include insurance although more research in this area may be warranted.

The permanent and term employees could be selected and trained to provide accurate and complementary interpretation of the resources. This would help to integrate the shuttle experience into the overall understanding of the resource by the visitors. This option is similar to the successful Lowell NHP program and offers interpretative advantages. For Morristown NHP an increase to base funding would need to be solicited to implement this scenario.

(2) Contracting to a third party to provide vehicles, drivers, and maintenance

Under this option, Morristown would operate the routes that service the Park units (again Park Circuits (Summer and Winter) and the Jockey Hollow Interpretive Loops) through a contract with a bus company. The annual contracted cost for one vehicle, a driver, and maintenance, as Adams NHP has done to date, can be 30 percent or more over the actual operation and maintenance costs for that vehicle. Given that the Morristown ATS system would likely either be a free or nominal fee service the contractor has no incentive to charge a lower cost to the Park. This option is the most costly for Morristown and the funds would need to come from the operating base budget. Adams NHP has seen a 54 percent increase in the annual cost for this service over the last five years. In addition, the pool of qualified bidders is quite limited. Of the three potential qualified bidders for Adams NHP, it was determined that their bids were within a few hundred dollars of each other. The capital cost of equipment is the reason why greater competition in the open market does not exist. The quality of drivers under contract varies and they do not provide any interpretation of the resource. Experience has shown that the ability for even a large contract operator to have a backup readily available is problematic. As there is no obvious source for a funding increase of this magnitude, this option is not seen to be viable.

(3) NPS buys the equipment, then obtains drivers and maintenance through a service contract(s)

In this scenario the NPS purchases the vehicles and contracts with a bus service to operate and maintain the vehicles. The assumption with this option is that the bus companies would be willing to contract with Morristown NHP for a significantly lower cost to the Park. Adams NHP assessed this option for running their rubber wheeled trolley and found that no cost savings would be realized under this option. The contractor would charge essentially the same amount for service support <u>with and without</u> the vehicles. The reason given is that they believe that their capital costs for their fleet is a fixed amount. If the same is true for the major bus companies in New Jersey, then no appreciable savings is estimated. It may be possible to solicit bids for this "driver/maintenance services only" and determine if small or new operations might be interested in such a contract. A possibility of savings may or may not exist if small or new operations were attracted to such a solicitation. There is some risk for a new operator taking over the service in terms of reliability of service. We expect that small operators may research this matter with larger operators and that the cost may not be dramatically reduced. Given the potential lack of savings with the large operators and uncertainty about the costs and reliability of a smaller or new operation this option is not seen to be viable.

(4) Partnering with a local government agency or a public-private organization

Several parks, most notably in the northeast Region, Acadia and Cape Cod National Seashore, have used this option successfully to operate bus systems that service the park visitor and the surrounding communities. Both Parks purchased vehicles for the ATS and turned them over to a public-private organization that receives operation and maintenance funds from Federal, state, and local agencies. The Park under this scenario is a critical stakeholder but is relieved of the day-to-day operations of a transit system. This option would work well to provide a unified system incorporating several route possibilities for both the Park and Morristown. Several transportation stakeholders have suggested that the Morristown Parking Authority may be such an entity willing to operate and maintain an ATS system.

The major roadblock to this option is funding. Recent discussions with the transportation stakeholders reveal no ready source of funds for operation and maintenance. There may be opportunities through NJT for Transportation Equity Act for the 21st Century (TEA-21) or FTA funds for initial start up capital. The NPS ATS program is looking to expand its funding capacity with the reauthorization of TEA-21 but that is not known to be certain. The first opportunity for Morristown to compete for capital funds for vehicles would be FY2004.

Volpe National Transportation Systems Center

5. NEXT STEPS

During a meeting of the Park staff and local stakeholders on October 3, 2001, to discuss ATS options, strong interest was generated by the participants to collaboratively proceed with the next phase for planning an ATS for Morristown. The Morristown Partnership has agreed to convene the next meeting of stakeholders to identify and address issues related to planning an ATS. Over the next few months, the stakeholders will need to consider the following questions:

- Who are all the stakeholders?
- How would local stakeholders formally partner with the Park to implement an ATS?
- What is the demand for an ATS in Morristown?
- How would the stakeholders test an ATS (e.g. pilot program)?
- Which routes would best serve Morristown?
- Which operating times would best serve Morristown?
- What are the funding sources?
- Who will pay the capital costs of an ATS?
- Who will pay the operating and maintenance costs of an ATS?
- Who will manage the ATS?
- Do the Federal government regulations allow private advertisement on their vehicles?

The participants informally listed the potential stakeholders of an ATS, including:

- Morristown NHP
- Morristown Partnership
- Morristown Parking Authority
- Morris County Department of Transportation
- TransOptions
- Morris County Park Commission
- New Jersey Transit
- New Jersey Department of Transportation
- Morristown Visitor Center
- Morristown Memorial Hospital
- Large Employers (e.g. AT&T)

In addition, the participants of the October 3, 2001 meeting suggested that interested stakeholders plan and conduct a pilot program to test the feasibility of an ATS for Morristown. The pilot program should test several routes and hours of operation.

Volpe National Transportation Systems Center

APPENDIX A - GLOSSARY OF TERMS

Arterial Route Signalized roadway that primarily serves through traffic and provides access to abutting properties as a secondary function

ATS Alternative Transportation System

ATS Station Transit station with physical features, such as bus turnarounds, pedestrian pathways, and shelters that facilitate vehicle operations and passenger use

Cycle Time Total time required by a single vehicle to complete a round trip of a transit route

Dwell Time The time a single vehicle spends at a station stop, measured as the time interval between its stopping and starting.

Headway Interval between successive arrivals of transit vehicles at an individual stop or station; service frequency

Tram Transit vehicle having features in common with a streetcar

VHT Vehicle hours traveled; measure of total time transit vehicles are in active service

VMT Vehicle miles traveled; measure of total distance traveled by vehicles in active service

Volpe National Transportation Systems Center

APPENDIX B – OPERATING PARAMETERS

Name	Operating Parameter	Unit of Measurement	Definition
Total Time	TT	minutes	ATS vehicle travel time at the prevailing road speeds
Dwell Time	DW	minutes	Aggregate dwell time
Terminal Layover	TL	minutes	Terminal layover time at the main transportation terminal or 'hub' to provide driver rest, and schedule recovery time which permits the succeeding vehicle run to be dispatched on time
Headway	h	minutes	Service headway or time interval between successive vehicles on the route as observed by a stationary observer at a stop
Stopping Time Penalty	τ	seconds	Acceleration and deceleration time penalty associated with a vehicle stopping at a station stop
Passenger Demand Rate	P	passengers per hour over the route	Aggregate demand rate between 'on' and 'off' station stops, averaged over all such pair of stops, on the route per hour
Station Stops	n	dimensionless	Number of station stops on the route
Service Processing Rate	μ	events per minute	Alighting and boarding passengers serviced per minute at a station stop
Fleet Size	N	dimensionless	Minimum number of ATS vehicles needed to operate a route
Capacity	c	passengers	ATS vehicle capacity in seated passengers
Span of Service	S	Hours	Span of operating service
Operating Season	OS	Days	Number of days in the operating season.

Volpe National Transportation Systems Center

APPENDIX C – CYCLE TIME AND MINIMUM FLEET SIZE CALCULATIONS

Once we can calculate the *cycle time* for each route in each ATS Configuration Option (see Section 3.1), in the absence of detailed usage or demand data we can postulate reasonable operating parameters (i.e., maximum passengers per vehicle, headway or frequency of service at each station stop, and span of service) and still derive proximate vehicle requirements. Likewise, we can derive a set of performance metrics for each route (vehicle hours traveled (VHT), vehicle miles traveled (VMT), vehicle trips per hour and per day, passenger capacity flow rate on the route). The performance metrics, in conjunction with proximate vehicle requirements, then permit cost estimates (admittedly rough) to be made.

Cycle Time (C) is the sum of ATS vehicle travel time, aggregate dwell time, aggregate time penalty for station stops, and terminal layover time. Therefore, we have:

$$C = TT + DW + n*\tau + TL \qquad (1)$$

Minimum fleet size (N) for a single fixed route transit system is determined by dividing the cycle time (C) by the headway (h)[47]:

$$N = [C/h] \text{ Greatest Integer} \qquad (2)$$

---

[47] See, e.g., S. Kikuchi, "Relationship between the Number of Stops and Headway for a Fixed-Route Transit System," *Trans. Res A* Vol. 19A, No. 1, pp. 65-71, 1985.

APPENDIX D – DWELL TIME CALCULATIONS

With the assumptions used for the Town-wide Loops, both the park and local circuit, we can compute approximate estimates for aggregate dwell time (DW).

Park Circuit

$$DW = [2*p * h/60]/\mu + [3 * 2 c]/\mu = 1/\mu [2*p*h/60 + 3*2*c] \qquad (3)$$

The above expression can be interpreted as follows: While we do not know explicitly the predicted ridership between each pair of stops, there is a generalized demand rate p. That portion that occurs within the operated headway interval equals (p*h/60). Each passenger that uses the service both boards and alights from the vehicle. Therefore, there are two station stop events associated with each passenger and the totality of such events, aggregated across all stops on the route, equals (2*p*h/60). These events can be processed at the rate of μ events per minute, given the ATS vehicle and station stop facility designs. Thus, the aggregate dwell time associated with the general level of ridership on the route is the first component of the above expression, namely $[2*p*h/60]/\mu$.

The second component is based on the planned nature and character of the service provided by the ATS Park Circuit. For the most part, visitors are collected at the 'common access points,' and transported to Washington Headquarters where they off-load for a tour of the Museum, Ford Mansion and grounds. A new group of visitors at Washington Headquarters, having completed their tour, load onto the ATS vehicle for transport to Fort Nonsense. The process repeats at both Fort Nonsense and at the Jockey Hollow Visitor Center. After visitation of Jockey Hollow, the passengers are transported back to, and distributed at the set of 'common access points'. During the summer operating season, some small fraction of passengers would alight and board at Lewis Morris Park, and/or Burnham Park, and Fosterfields on the return journey to the center of Morristown[48]. Thus at each of the three Park units there is a full passenger interchange of the ATS vehicle, yielding 2c events in the peak (and 2c', c' = 0.6 c, in the off-peak). With the three Park units, there are 3*2c events. These events too can only be processed at a rate of μ. Therefore, the aggregate dwell time associated with this type of operation as just described is equal to $[3*2c]/\mu$.

Local Circuit

$$DW = [2*p * h/60]/\mu + [0.5* c]/\mu = 1/\mu [2*p*h/60 + 0.5*c] \qquad (4a) \text{ Peak Hours}$$

$$DW = [2*p *h/60]/\mu \qquad (4b) \text{ Off-Peak Hours}$$

As for the ATS Park Circuit, the first component of the dwell time represents a general aggregate estimate based on the general level of ridership along the route. The second component adds the incremental dwell time at the maximum load point (i.e., the AT&T Corporate Center) during the peak hours. Note that there is only a one-way interchange (i.e., passengers either alight or board) during the peak hours.

---

[48] This portion of dwell time is already captured in the first component of expression (3).

Volpe National Transportation Systems Center

www.ingramcontent.com/pod-product-compliance
Lightning Source LLC
Chambersburg PA
CBHW081800170526
45167CB00008B/3265